© 2024 BuchBlick

Autor:
Lorenzo De Luca

Publisher:
Buchblick Verlag
represented by
Andrey Bernhart
Bahnhofstraße 17
6824 Schlins
Austria

ISBN:
9798326255730

USELESS FACTS

ABOUT THE

ROMAN EMPIRE

TABLE OF CONTENTS

I

LIFE IN THE ROMAN EMPIRE

Rome began as a small settlement and gradually grew into a city with public buildings, streets, temples and aqueducts. The first houses in Rome were simple huts made of mud bricks and thatched roofs. These materials were initially sufficient, but proved to be highly flammable, which led to frequent fires in the growing city. At that time, nobody knew how big this small village would grow.

SWAMPY BEGINNINGS

The original area on which Rome was built was actually swampy and infertile. The early Romans had to carry out extensive drainage work to make the land habitable. There are many reasons why such unsuitable land was chosen to build a settlement. Among other things, the surrounding area was very fertile, the 7 hills on which Rome was built were ideal for defense, it had a central location in Italy and was the scene of many legends and myths, which was of great importance to the Romans of the time.

WOW, STREETS!

The first roads in Rome were unpaved and were simply formed through regular use. It was only much later that the Romans began to pave their roads, starting with the Via Appia, one of the first and most important Roman roads. The road was originally built to provide soldiers with a convenient and much faster connection to the southern areas under Rome's control. Of course, traveling on paved roads is faster than on uneven dirt roads, which was a clear strategic advantage for the early Roman army. Streets were initially dirt paths. As the city developed, some streets were covered with gravel or stones to improve durability and usability.

THE CLOACA MAXIMA

One of the most impressive engineering feats in ancient Rome was the construction of the Cloaca Maxima, a huge sewer that was used to drain the marshes in the valley of the Roman Forum and is considered one of the first sewage systems in the world. It was built in the 6th century B.C., and its enduring functionality showcases the advanced engineering capabilities of the Romans. Remarkably, parts of this ancient sewer system are still in use today.

A ROME WITHOUT LAWS

In the Roman royal period from 753 BC to 509 BC, there were no written laws. Instead, legal decisions were transmitted orally and were heavily dependent on the traditions and judgment of the kings. This reliance on oral tradition and royal discretion meant that legal outcomes could vary significantly, reflecting the personal authority and interpretation of each ruler.

FISTS INSTEAD OF GLADIATORS

Fist fights were very popular with the Romans several centuries before the first gladiator fights. In the broadest sense, it can be compared to modern boxing, although there were no real rules and spectators expected the fighters to fight to the death. So the Romans have always been fans of life-or-death contests.

EARLY LUXURY CONSUMPTION

Despite their relatively isolated location and predominantly agricultural economy, the early Romans imported luxury goods such as ivory, spices and silk from far and wide, demonstrating the early trading spirit and desire for exotic goods. The Romans always presented themselves as very sophisticated, were very hygienic and appreciated luxury. This is also a stark contrast to their brutality when it comes to competitions and entertainment.

ROMAN LUXURY

Fashion and jewelry: Luxurious clothing and jewelry were important status symbols. Wealthy Romans wore garments made of fine fabrics such as silk and adorned themselves with gold, precious stones and other valuable materials.

Art and sculpture: Wealthy Romans adorned their homes and public spaces with works of art, sculptures, mosaics and other decorative objects that often showed Greek and Etruscan influences.

Construction of villas and gardens: Wealthy Romans invested in magnificent villas, often in picturesque locations such as on the coast or in the countryside. Of course, they also lived in them, but they were primarily there to show off to other Romans.

Public baths and thermal baths: The Romans had an early awareness of personal hygiene and wellness. Even the lower social classes had access to public baths in order to experience a little luxury.

THE BIRTH OF THE GLADIATORS

The first gladiator fights took place in 264 BC. They were originally fights held in honor of deceased nobles. The children or relatives of the deceased organized private fights in which mostly convicted criminals or prisoners of war had to fight each other to the death. These early fights had a strong ritual significance and served to honor the ancestors with the blood of the fallen. The first known gladiatorial event was held by Decimus Junius Brutus Scaeva in honor of his deceased father. Three pairs of gladiators (thraeces) fought in a tomb or a small fighting area. These fights took place to honor the memory of the deceased and to appease the dead with the blood of the fighters.

BRUTAL TRADITION

Over time, gladiator fights became increasingly popular and developed into a form of public enter-tainment organized by statesmen and later by the Roman state. They eventually took place in specially built arenas, of which the Colosseum in Rome is the most famous example. Gladiator fights became an integral part of Roman culture and society.

TOP TRAINED SLAVES

As gladiatorial skills developed, slaves were increasingly trained for this purpose. These slaves were trained in special schools (ludi gladiatorii) to perform in combat and entertain spectators. Prisoners of war and criminals were still used as gladiators, but trained slaves were later more popular as they survived much longer and could offer the spectators a "better show". Over time, the spectacle of gladiatorial combat became a highly organized and regulated form of entertainment.

VOLUNTEER FIGHTERS

In addition to these forced fighters, there were also volunteers who competed as gladiators, often motivated by the promise of fame, money and, in the case of slaves, the possibility of gaining their freedom. These volunteers could be either free citizens or slaves who decided to take on the hard and dangerous life of a gladiator. For slaves, this was one of the few ways to earn their freedom. You had to survive for a long time, win several battles and gain great popularity among the people to be able to initiate this process of release. However, only very few cases actually resulted in a release. If someone was freed, they were given the title of "freedman", which gave them some rights, but they were not yet true citizens.

THE MOST FAMOUS GLADIATOR CLASSES

Murmillo: Equipped with a large shield (scutum), a short sword (gladius) or a dagger, a helmet with a distinctive herringbone crest and greaves.

Thraex (Thracian): Armed with a small, rectangular or curved shield (parma), a short, curved sword (sica) suitable for close combat, a helmet with a side plume and greaves.

Hoplomachus: Inspired by Greek hoplites, he carried a lance (hasta), a short sword, a round shield, a helmet, often with a crown of feathers, and greaves for protection.

Retiarius: Fought with a net (rete), a trident, a small dagger and sometimes a shoulder plate (galerus). He wore no helmet or large armor, which gave him mobility.

Secutor: Equipped similarly to the Murmillo, but with a smoother helmet without a crest to offer the Retiarius fewer points of attack. The Secutor hunted the Retiarius in a fight that was staged as a hunting game.

Samnite: An earlier class equipped with a long shield, a visored helmet, a gladius and greaves. This class later became less popular and was replaced by others.

Dimachaerus: Fought with two swords, one in each hand. These gladiators were known for their skill and ability to fight with two weapons at the same time.

Equites: Roman knights who were mounted at the beginning of their battle and fought with a spear and a small round shield. They often began the battle on horseback before continuing on foot.

GLADIATOR CLASSES

Gladiators in ancient Rome were equipped with a variety of weapons, depending on their fighting class. Each gladiator class had its own equipment and fighting technique. In addition to the 8 listed, there were many more. A total of 22 clearly defined classes are recognized as gladiators today. The different classes also had different opponents. Some classes only fought against gladiators of the same class, others never fought against their own class and some staged shows such as Secutor and Retiarius.

OWNER AND TRAINER

The gladiators were trained and managed by a "lanista" (owner and trainer of gladiators).A gladiator who was popular with the public became more valuable, and the lanista could send him to the arena for a higher fee.This popularity and financial value could give a gladiator more influence and negotiating power, which could provide opportunities for release.Fundamentally, however, gladiators were seen as property and a means of earning money.The lanista sent them into battle, speculated on their victory and could demand even more money for their gladiator the next time.This principle still exists today, for example in illegal underground dog fights.

THE COLOSSEUM

The Colosseum was built between 70 and 80 AD under the emperors Vespasian and Titus, members of the Flavian dynasty, which earned it the name "Flavian Amphitheater". It was not given the name Colosseum until the Middle Ages. It could hold between 50,000 and 80,000 spectators, making it the largest amphitheater of its time. Even by today's standards, with this number of spectators it would pass for a large soccer stadium.

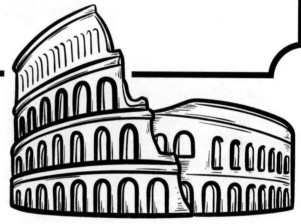

MASTERFUL ARCHITECTURE

Below the arena was a complex system of corridors and cells known as the hypogeum, where gladiators, slaves and animals were kept before the events. It also had advanced technical features such as a retractable velarium (solar sail) that protected spectators from the sun. Naumachia (re-enacted sea battles) also took place in the Colosseum, as the arena could be flooded in the early days.

FAR MORE THAN GLADIATORS

As mentioned, naval battles and other events also took place in the Colosseum. For example, public executions were often carried out there, there were animal fights and many other forms of entertainment. The idea that the Colosseum was used purely for gladiator fights is therefore too short-sighted.

SYMBOL OF POWER

The Colosseum symbolized the power and prosperity of the Roman Empire as well as the engineering and architectural skills of the Romans. The Romans were known not only for impressing their people with buildings and their advanced infrastructure, but also for showing off to other peoples. In its day, the Colosseum was definitely also a means of demonstrating their superiority to others.

DECAY AND PRESERVATION

After the fall of the Roman Empire, the Colosseum was partially looted and its materials were reused for other construction projects. Despite decay and earthquakes, it has been partially preserved and continues to attract millions of tourists as a ruin. Today, the Colosseum is a UNESCO World Heritage Site and a symbol of Italy's cultural and historical heritage.

CHARIOT RACES

Roman chariot racing was one of the most popular forms of entertainment in Ancient Rome and took place mainly in the Circus Maximus, a large racecourse built especially for these events. The chariot racers, known as aurigae, were often slaves or freedmen who trained extensively to master the dangerous and thrilling sport.

CIRCUS MAXIMUS

The Circus Maximus, the largest racecourse in ancient Rome, could accommodate around 150,000 to 250,000 spectators. By comparison, the largest soccer stadium in the world can only accommodate just over half that number. It was 600 meters long and 140 meters wide, was the main center for chariot races and other public games and was used for these purposes until the 6th century AD. According to legend, a Roman king erected a wooden grandstand as early as 580 BC, which is recognized by many as the first version of the Circus. Under Caesar and later Augustus, the Circus was significantly expanded. Augustus then erected the first obelisk (today's "Obelisco Flaminio") in the middle of the track.

FACTS ABOUT
THE CHARIOT RACES

Enormous rewards: Some of the most famous charioteers earned enormous sums that could dwarf the earnings of successful athletes today.

Betting: Even back then, many people bet on the outcome of chariot races and made (or lost) a lot of money doing so.

Short careers: Despite their potential for fame and fortune, the careers of charioteers were often short and dangerous. Accidents were frequent and many drivers did not survive their racing days.

Political advertising: Politicians often used chariot races to promote themselves by sponsoring teams or organizing spectacular races to win the favour of the people.

THUMBS UP!

Modern films and pop culture have propagated the image that thumbs up and thumbs down could be used by the people to signal whether defeated gladiators should be killed or spared. While there is no clear historical evidence about the exact gestures, it was indeed the case that the audience could often decide the fate of the losers. Some historians argue that in ancient Rome the thumb inwards or pressed into the fist (pollice compresso) was actually used as a sign of mercy, while a raised arm or 'thumbs up' may have been the signal for the death blow.

BREAD AND GAMES

"Bread and games" (in Latin "panem et circenses") is an expression originally used by the Roman poet Juvenal to describe the strategy of Roman emperors to win the favor of the people by distributing grain (bread) free of charge and staging spectacular mass entertainment (games). These included impressive scales races, theatrical performances and brutal gladiator fights. This policy served to ensure public satisfaction and minimize potential unrest among the population of Rome.

MAN AND WOMAN

In a legal sense, men had far more freedoms and rights than women. Free men of legal age enjoyed full Roman citizenship, which granted them political, social and economic privileges. Women, on the other hand, were under the legal guardianship of men, initially their father and later their husband or a close male relative. Although they could own property, they were severely restricted in their legal abilities, such as concluding contracts or taking independent legal action. One example is inheritance. No matter how old you were, male children were given priority over female children in most cases. Women were also excluded from direct participation in political life.

EDUCATIONAL DIFFERENCES

Education for boys often included rhetoric, philosophy, literature, and physical training to prepare them for roles in public and political life. Girls were mostly educated at home, focusing on household, weaving, and other skills to prepare them for their roles as wives and mothers. However, some women from wealthy families received a more comprehensive education, somewhat similar to that of men, including lessons in reading, writing, and even managing estates. Additionally, these women might have access to private tutors, allowing them to explore subjects like music, poetry, and philosophy in greater depth.

FAMILY AND MARRIAGE

Men had a dominant role in the family and were the main decision-makers. They had legal authority (patria potestas) over all family members. Women were primarily responsible for running the household, raising the children, and maintaining the familia (family and household). In wealthy families, these tasks were often carried out by slaves, while the matrona (housewife) had a more supervisory role. Some women in prominent families also engaged in social and political activities through their influence.

PUBLIC LIFE

Men were active in political, military, and public life and had access to political offices and public duties. Military service was an essential part of a man's life, typically beginning at age 17 and lasting 16 to 20 years. Women were largely excluded from formal political life, but they exerted considerable influence in social and religious spheres through roles in cults and ceremonies, especially those dedicated to female deities. As Vestal Virgins or priestesses, women could attain significant power and respect, maintaining sacred fires and conducting important rites believed to ensure Rome's prosperity. Additionally, women from influential families often acted as patrons and advisors, indirectly shaping political and social dynamics through their connections and counsel.

COMPARISON WITH TODAY

Due to the strong religious focus, the clear division of male and female gender roles, the decades of military service for men and the completely different way of life, it is almost impossible to compare today and then. Both men and women had their own roles back then and many were happy with them. While women had fewer rights, they also had far fewer duties. They were also happy that they didn't have to do 20 years of military service like men, which was often half or at least a third of a lifetime back then. On the other hand, there were also many women who were treated badly by their husbands and had no way of reporting it or leaving the marriage. Today, men and women enjoy a completely different level of rights and freedoms. If the Romans of the time had been told about what our modern cohabitation of men and women looks like today, they would not only have been overwhelmed, they simply would not have been able to understand many things because the realities are so incredibly far apart.

SOCIAL CLASSES

In ancient Rome, there were different social classes that determined the political, social and economic life of the city. The main categories of Roman society were the patricians, the plebeians, the equesters (knights), the slaves and the freedmen. In addition, the status of a Roman citizen was of great importance and brought with it special rights and duties.

THE "UPPER CLASS"

The patricians were the aristocratic upper class and formed the political and religious elite of Rome. Their power was based on traditional inheritance rights, land ownership and political influence. They had exclusive access to most priestly offices and state magistracies.

THE POWER OF SUCH OFFICES

The Roman deities, which we will learn more about later, played a significant role in the Roman Empire. Those who held priestly offices had incredible power and political influence. We often think of them as ordinary priests in our modern world, but in fact, offices were big status symbols back then, even bigger than fast cars or beautiful houses here today.

STATE MAGISTRATES

Initially, the patricians were the only Romans who could hold high political offices such as the consulship (the highest level of office in the Roman Republic), the praetorship (responsible for the administration of justice) and the aedilate (responsible for the administration of the city and the organization of public games). Over time, these exclusive rights were gradually eroded so that plebeians could also gain access to many of these offices. This process led to a more democratic and balanced political structure, in which office was awarded according to merit rather than birthright.

ORDINARY CITIZENS

The plebeians made up the vast majority of the Roman people and were originally ordinary citizens without the aristocratic privileges mentioned above. They were farmers, craftsmen, merchants and soldiers. Social advancement was only possible to a very limited extent, for example through economic success or marriage. Similar to our societies today, the plebeians were able to work their way up through hard work and become economically successful, but this was a difficult and lengthy process. Despite their wealth, they did not receive any aristocratic privileges.

MILITARY AND MARRIAGE

Serving in the Roman army offered plebeians the opportunity to achieve glory and honor on the battlefield and was a way to rise socially. Successful military careers could lead to recognition, wealth and sometimes a certain amount of political influence. The "Lex Canuleia" of 445 BC also allowed marriages between patricians and plebeians, which paved the way for social advancement through family connections. It was therefore possible to marry into higher social classes and thus secure a higher social status and far-reaching privileges for oneself or at least one's future children.

EQUESTER (KNIGHT)

The term "equites" comes from "equus", the Latin word for horse. In the early days of the Roman Republic, knights were actually mounted warriors who came from wealthy families who could afford to maintain a horse for military purposes. With the professionalization of the military and the expansion of the Roman Empire, the role of the knights changed. They increasingly became a class of wealthy citizens who were active in trade, industry and finance. Knights had the privilege of sitting in the front rows at public games, which underlined their high social status.

LIVING PROPERTY (SLAVES)

Slaves had no rights and were regarded as property. They often came to Rome as prisoners of war or were traded in the Mediterranean. Their living conditions varied greatly depending on the area in which they were used and how their owners treated them. The children of slaves, known as "vernae", were also born as slaves and eventually formed a significant part of the slave population.

SLAVE ≠ SLAVE

The roles and tasks of slaves in ancient Rome were extremely varied and ranged from hard physical labour in the mines and fields to specialized and trusted positions such as teachers, doctors, artists or household managers.Some slaves could work their way up to become administrators (vilici) or overseers (actors), who bore significant responsibility for the business and property affairs of their masters. However, they remained extremely restricted in terms of freedom and were seen as property, although of course it made a big difference whether you were forced to work in a mine or teach children as a learned slave.

PILLAR OF THE ECONOMY

Slaves, their work and their trade were an important part of the Roman economy. Freeing all slaves at once would have led to the complete collapse of Roman society. Furthermore, owning slaves was not a rarity or a privilege reserved for the wealthy or aristocratic classes.

In fact, owning slaves was widespread across all social classes. However, the extent of slave ownership varied considerably depending on the wealth and status of an individual or family.

FREEDMEN

Freedmen were former slaves who had gained their freedom. They enjoyed certain rights, such as the right to marry and trade, but were excluded from some public offices and priesthoods. They still formed a class below the plebeians, the ordinary citizens. Like the plebeians, freedmen could build up considerable wealth if they were economically successful. They were also allowed to marry into higher social classes and thus earn additional social status and privileges. However, this only happened very rarely, as the other classes had many prejudices against them.

ROMAN CITIZEN STATUS

To be considered a Roman citizen, one usually had to be born into citizenship, or one could attain citizenship through the process of manumission (release from slavery), marriage, adoption or as a reward for special services to the state. Roman citizens had certain privileges, including the right to vote, hold certain offices, enter into legal contracts and make use of Roman law. Freedmen often had no citizen status, which still restricted them in many areas of Roman society.

POOR MEETS RICH

There were few places and situations where the different social classes all crossed paths at the same time. Roman baths, however, were open to all social classes, which led to rare interactions between patricians, plebeians, freedmen and even slaves. There were also separate areas in many baths that segregated according to status, but it was not uncommon to be confronted with people of a different class in baths and to interact with them. This underlines once again how important and natural the luxury of heated baths and wellness was for the Roman population, as even the lowest class was accepted there.

FACTS ABOUT THE
ROMAN POPULATION

Patricians and plebeians in the army: In the early phases of Roman history, military units were strictly organized according to social classes. Patricians served as officers, while the plebeians formed the rank and file.

Special way of eating: In rich Roman homes, family members ate in a reclining position on dining beds (triclinia), while slaves and servants stood or ate on simple seats.

Salt as a salary: Some historians believe that the word "salary" comes from the Latin word "salarium", which refers to payments to Roman soldiers, some of which were made in salt.

Fake family trees: Some up-and-coming Roman families created fake family trees to feign noble origins and increase their social status.

CITY FULL OF PROSTITUTES

Prostitution in ancient Rome was a widespread and legally recognized activity, but it was viewed rather negatively by society. It was seen as a necessary evil that fulfilled certain social and sexual needs, but at the same time was held in low esteem. You could compare the reputation of prostitutes with their reputation here today: Legal, but if your own daughter did it, you wouldn't feel good about it.

STATE REGULATED

Prostitution was a normal trade in the Roman Empire and was regulated. Prostitutes (meretrices) often had to register and pay taxes. There were also different classes of prostitutes, from slaves who were forced into prostitution by their owners to independent freelancers who worked in this industry to earn a living. There were also male prositutes. Male prostitutes, known as "meretrices" if they were slaves and "scorta" if they were free, served both male and female clients. They worked in various venues, including brothels, private homes, and public baths.

BAD REPUTATION

Although prostitution was recognized as a profession, prostitutes were socially stigmatized. They were considered "infames" (people with a bad reputation) and had limited rights.

WIDESPREAD AND NORMAL

Despite their negative reputation, men from all social classes, including the upper classes, regularly sought out prostitutes. The use of prostitutes was more widespread than it is today and was seen as a normal part of the male sexual experience. Although, as in modern times, people did not like to talk about it openly and women in particular were not held in high esteem if involved in such professions, it was normal for men to use these services. The Roman faith lacked commandments, such as our Christian "no sex before marriage," which would have made the moral boundaries of such activities clear. Instead, wives were expected to be faithful to their husbands, while it was common and socially acceptable for men to consort with prostitutes or slaves, even in spite of their marital commitments. This double standard highlights the differing expectations and freedoms granted to men and women in ancient Roman society.

EXCESSIVE ORGIES

The idea of orgies in ancient Rome is usually very exaggerated. Historically, orgies were nothing normal in Rome, but rather a sexual perversion of some emperors or other powerful people. It was therefore certain personalities in Roman history who celebrated great orgies and not the Roman people in general.

CLOTHING AND ITS SIGNIFICANCE

Clothes make the man - the Romans in Ancient Rome were also convinced of this. Compared to many Germanic tribes, the Romans' style of dress went far beyond mere functionality. Clothing denoted status, social standing and religious positions. Those who knew how to dress had a higher reputation and often more influence within their class

THE TUNIC

The tunic was the everyday garment worn by men and women of all social classes. It was a simple, shirt-like garment that reached down to the knees and was made of wool, linen or cotton. The tunic could be sleeveless or have short to long sleeves, depending on status, fashion and personal preference. Due to its practicality and comfort, the tunic was the standard garment for everyday wear, both at home and at work.

SHOE FASHION

The type of sandals or shoes one wore also signaled social status. Patricians often wore calfskin shoes, while slaves had to walk barefoot or wear simple sandals.

THE TOGA

The toga was a symbol of the Roman bourgeoisie and was only worn by free Roman citizens. It was a large, heavy woolen garment that was wrapped around the body in an intricate manner and served as a sign of social status and belonging to Roman society. Due to its size and complexity, the toga was less practical and was mainly worn on public occasions, ceremonies, political meetings, or court hearings. The toga was usually white, but certain variations, such as the toga praetexta with a purple border, were reserved for special social groups, such as senators and priests. The toga pulla, a rather dark toga, was mostly worn for mourning and funerals, similar to our black clothing at funerals. Additionally, the toga candida, a bright white toga, was worn by political candidates to signify their purity and intentions.

LENGTH IS IMPORTANT

In Rome, the length of the toga was a status symbol. While the richer citizens wore long, elaborate togas that touched the ground, poorer citizens wore shorter togas that were more practical for physical labor.

TIME-CONSUMING CHANGING OF CLOTHES

Putting on the toga was complicated and often required the help of a slave. It was wrapped around the body, usually over a tunic, and draped so that a kind of bow or fold (sinus) fell across the chest and a wide strip of fabric (umbo) hung down. The correct draping of the toga was so important that it was often seen as a sign of a man's virtue and character. A toga that is not worn properly is like going to a job interview in swimming trunks today.

UNDERWEAR

Romans of both sexes wore a type of undergarment known as a "subligaculum", a simple form of shorts or loincloth under their tunics.

CLOTHING IN THE BATHS

On arrival at the baths, the Romans usually undressed down to the subligaculum and went into the bathing area. As in our indoor baths, there were lockers to store their clothes. Romans were usually naked while bathing. Nudity was culturally accepted in public Roman baths and was not considered indecent. In private baths, especially for mixed use, there was also a kind of bathing robe.

FACTS ABOUT THE
ROMAN CLOTHING

Colorful fashion: Despite the classic image of Romans in white robes, the Romans loved to wear colorful clothing. Women in particular wore tunics in vibrant, bright colors.

Washing clothes with urine: In ancient Rome, urine was used as a cleaning agent for clothes due to its ammonia-containing properties to remove stains from garments and make them brighter.

Perfumed clothing: Romans often used fragrant oils and perfumes, not only on their skin, but they also soaked their clothes in them to give off a pleasant smell and emphasize their social status.

Fashion police: The "zensor " in ancient Rome had the task of monitoring public morals, which included monitoring the clothing and jewelry of citizens to prevent excesses and inappropriate behavior.

EDUCATION

Education began early for Roman children, especially those from wealthy families, and included learning reading, writing, arithmetic and often Greek, which was considered the language of scholarship. Boys continued their formal education to study rhetoric, philosophy, law and sometimes military tactics, which prepared them for public and political roles. Early on, the boys were taken along to political meetings and banquets in order to make a good impression on important people. Girls, as already mentioned, were usually trained more in skills useful to the role of wife.

FAMILY AND SOCIAL LIFE

Young people spent a lot of time with their families and were introduced to the family duties and social status of their families. Social events, religious ceremonies and public festivals played an important role in the lives of young people. These occasions provided opportunities to strengthen social bonds and build important networks for their future. Physical training was also a central part of leisure time, especially for boys, as it promoted physical fitness, general health and later readiness for military service.

RHETORIC AND MORALS

In a society like Rome's, where public speaking and political activity were highly valued, rhetorical education was central to preparing young men for roles in public and political life. This underlines the relevance of the culture of discourse in Ancient Rome and how important it was for them to listen to different opinions and debate them openly. Moral education was also a central element of Roman education, with values such as discipline, respect for authority, loyalty to the family and to the state being emphasized. Young people from wealthier families in particular were expected to grow up to be educated and independent-minded individuals, each of whom had the potential to take on an important social role or make a career in the military. Cities in the center of the Roman Empire, above all Rome itself, had many decades, even centuries, of long periods of peace, as a result of which a society of eloquent politicians developed in the higher social classes

COMING OF AGE FOR GIRLS

While young men went off to war, it was normal for girls to marry at a young age, which marked their transition from "girl" to woman.

THE LIFE OF YOUNG PEOPLE
IN THE ROMAN EMPIRE

Just like today, ball sports were incredibly popular in Ancient Rome. From simple catching and throwing games to more complex team games that required skill and coordination.

Roman children liked to play with dolls, which were often made of clay, wood or fabric, similar to children today.These dolls could be very detailed and artistic.

Board games such as "latrunculi" (a game similar to chess or a checkers) and "tabula" (a type of backgammon) were also popular.

Evidence suggests that bullying in schools was already a problem in Ancient Rome. For example, rich children could show off with expensive clothes, similar to today with brands.

From an early age, boys in particular took part in banquets and ceremonies in order to learn how to interact with adults and to attract the attention of important personalities through their behavior.

LIFE IN GENERAL
IN THE ROMAN EMPIRE

Both Roman men and women used cosmetics such as skin creams, perfumes and hair dyes. There were even recipes for toothpaste containing ingredients such as eggshells and honey.

Roman politicians wore a white toga (toga candida) during election campaigns to present themselves as candidates (candidatus), which literally means "bleached" or "whitened". This practice is the origin of today's word "candidate".

In Ancient Rome, images of phalli were widely used as amulets and were regarded as symbols of luck, fertility and protection from the evil eye.Esotericism was therefore already popular with the Romans.

Rich Romans often had extravagant dishes such as flamingo and peacock tongues. They organized opulent banquets where the display of abundance was almost as important as the food itself.

THE ROMAN DEITIES

As in many cultures of the time, deities played a major role. While the state and religion are clearly separated today, this was much less clear back then. Whoever had religious power in Rome also had enormous political power. The origin of Roman deities is a combination of indigenous Italic traditions, the influence of neighboring cultures, especially the Greeks and Etruscans, and the later adaptation of deities from the conquered territories.

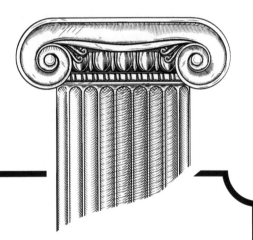

ITALIC GODS

The earliest Roman deities were often natural and spiritual beings associated with specific places, states and human activities. They were considered numina (plural of numen), indicating a spiritual force or presence at work in the natural world and in daily life. Examples of such deities are Janus, the god of doors and transitions, and Vesta, the goddess of hearth fires and domestic life.

ZEUS AND JUPITER

In the course of intensive interaction with the Greek world, especially after the conquest of Greek territories in the 3rd and 2nd centuries BC, the Romans adopted many aspects of Greek religion and mythology. Many Roman deities were identified with their Greek counterparts and sometimes merged, which is known as Interpretatio Romana. For example, the Greek god Zeus was equated with the Roman Jupiter, and similar connections existed between Hera and Juno, Poseidon and Neptune, Aphrodite and Venus and so on. Philosophically, the Romans had already borrowed a lot from the Greeks, which is why it was logical to adopt their gods as well.

PLANETS?

The Roman gods are not named after the planets, but the reverse is true: the planets are named after the Roman gods. However, it was not the Romans but the Greeks who made the connection between deities and celestial bodies. The Greeks named the planets after their gods, based on their characteristics and the movement of the planets in the sky. This tradition was continued by the Romans when they equated the Greek deities with their own and thus also gave the planets Roman names.

THE ROMAN DEITIES

Jupiter (Iuppiter): The king of the gods, god of the sky and lightning, who represented divine authority and law.

Juno (Iuno): The wife of Jupiter, goddess of marriage and childbirth, and one of the most important patron saints of Rome.

Minerva: Goddess of wisdom, war, art, schools and crafts, often equated with Athena in Greek mythology.

Mars: God of war, agriculture and the progenitor of the Roman people, father of Romulus and Remus according to legends.

Venus: Goddess of love, beauty and fertility, associated with the Greek goddess Aphrodite.

Apollo: God of light, healing, the plague, music, art and prophecy, adopted from the Greeks without a change of name.

Diana: Goddess of hunting, animals and the moon, corresponds to the Greek goddess Artemis.

Neptune (Neptunus): God of the seas, rivers, springs and horses, identified with the Greek Poseidon.

Vulcan (Vulcanus): God of fire, metallurgy and blacksmithing, associated with the Greek Hephaestus.

Pluto (Pluton): God of the underworld and god of wealth, especially mineral wealth such as gold and precious stones. He corresponds to the Greek Hades.

THE GOLDEN AGE

In this mythological period, people lived in harmony with nature, without labor or conflict, and abundance was so great that no one needed to farm or trade. There was no need for laws or punishments, as all people were inherently just and good. This age is often described as a paradisiacal state in which man and nature existed in perfect harmony, without the need for labor, war or social injustice.

THE FALL OF SATURN

Saturn is said to have ruled over Italy during this Golden Age. According to mythology, Saturn's reign ended when he was overthrown by his son Jupiter, marking a transition from the mythological age of the gods to the historical age of man. With the fall of Saturn, the Golden Age ended and the reign of the Olympian gods began under the leadership of Jupiter. These ages include the Silver, Bronze and Iron Ages, with the Iron Age seen as the age of human history, characterized by work, conflict and moral decline.

THE ROMAN PANTHEON

The Roman pantheon refers to the entirety of the deities worshipped in ancient Rome. It included both major gods, who were often Olympian deities with Greek equivalents, as well as a multitude of smaller, local and specialized deities. What is special about the Roman pantheon is that it was strongly based on integration. The Romans regularly incorporated deities from other cultures into their pantheon and often gave them the same status as their own gods. Through the many conquests of the Romans over the course of time, the pantheon became a comprehensive collection of the most diverse deities and cultures.

THE RISE OF CHRISTIANITY

Christianity began as a Jewish sect in the 1st century AD and gradually spread throughout the Roman Empire. Initially, it was seen as a threat and subversive force by the Roman authorities. Despite persecution, the Christian community grew, partly because of its inclusive message, its organizational structure and the appeal of a monotheistic (there is only one God), personal religion that promised salvation and an afterlife.

THE ROMAN INVENTIVE GENIUS

The Romans were exceptional engineers and architects whose ingenuity and technical skills enabled them to create impressive buildings and infrastructure that still stand today. Their ability to develop advanced technologies such as underfloor heating, aqueducts and other impressive structures was based on a combination of practical knowledge, scientific understanding and a strong system of state organization.

ENGINEERING

The Romans developed and perfected the use of concrete (opus caementicium), which enabled them to build larger and more durable structures than ever before. This material was crucial in the construction of many of their monumental buildings, including the Pantheon in Rome with its famous dome. They were also pioneers in the use of technical aids such as cranes, winches and sophisticated waterlifting machines used in large construction projects. As the Romans cared enormously about the cityscape and their public baths, temples, theaters and the like, they eventually perfected the planning and construction of these facilities.

THE PANTHEON (BUILDING)

The Pantheon, a building named after the great collection of Roman deities, is an ancient structure that was originally built as a temple to all the gods of the ancient Roman faith. It is one of the best-preserved buildings of ancient Rome and an architectural masterpiece, known for its impressive dome and harmonious proportions. At the front of the Pantheon is a classical portico with Corinthian columns leading into the rotunda, a cylindrical structure crowned with a huge dome. The dome was an architectural innovation in antiquity and is still the largest unreinforced concrete dome in the world today.

THE ROMAN AQUEDUCTS

The Roman aqueducts were remarkable feats of engineering designed to transport fresh water over long distances from the springs to the urban centers, especially Rome. These structures are a testament to Roman ingenuity and their understanding of engineering and hydrology.

INCREDIBLE LENGTHS

Some of the longest aqueducts, such as the Aqua Marcia in Rome, were over 90 kilometers long. The Aqua Appia, one of the earliest Roman aqueducts, was over 16 kilometers long, and the Aqua Traiana even reached over 60 kilometers. The network of aqueducts that supplied Rome had a total length of over 500 kilometers.

CHALLENGES

The main challenge in the construction of aqueducts was the need to ensure a continuous and gentle slope so that the water could flow by gravity. This required precise surveying work and a deep understanding of hydraulics. The Romans had to overcome natural obstacles such as valleys, mountains and rivers. They built impressive bridges and supporting structures to keep the aqueducts at the required level. The aqueducts were mostly underground to protect the water from contamination and minimize loss through evaporation. Where this was not possible, they were routed along imposing arcades (see sketch on the left), which remain iconic landscape elements to this day.

IMPORTANCE OF AQUEDUCTS

Aqueducts were crucial to the development and growth of Roman cities as they provided a reliable water supply for drinking water, public baths, latrines and even for street cleaning and industrial purposes. They were also a symbol of the prosperity and technical superiority of the Roman Empire and played an important role in Roman culture and politics.

UNDERFLOOR HEATING

The Romans are considered the inventors of underfloor heating. The so-called hypocaust was a system for heating buildings, especially public baths and wealthy private homes, by warm air circulating through cavities under the floors and in the walls. This was an early form of central heating that used fires in a furnace (praefurnium) to heat air, which was then circulated through the building to efficiently heat rooms. The sketch below shows how this design was used to heat a public bath. With the fall of the Roman Empire, however, this technique of ancient underfloor heating fell into oblivion again. It was not until the 20th century that this type of underfloor heating became fashionable again and is often imitated in the construction of new houses today. This shows once again how far ahead of their time the Roman engineers were.

FACTS ABOUT
LIFE IN ANCIENT ROME

Brushing teeth with urine: As with laundry, Romans sometimes used human urine as mouthwash and to clean their teeth.

Road traffic in Rome: Due to the heavy traffic in the ancient city of Rome, carriages were often prohibited during the day. Most of the transportation of goods and the movements of the rich in their carriages took place at night.

Fast food in ancient Rome: There were numerous street stalls and eateries known as "thermopolia", where citizens could buy quickly prepared food, similar to today's fast food restaurants.

Graffiti: Just like today, graffiti was everywhere in ancient Rome. Walls in Pompeii are full of graffiti, ranging from election advertisements to everyday gossip and obscenities.

THE ROMAN ARMY

THE ROMAN ARMY

The Roman army was one of the most powerful and successful armed forces in human history and played a decisive role in the expansion and preservation of the Roman Empire. Their success was based on perfect organization, extreme discipline, and the ability to adapt to the most diverse conditions of war.

CENTERPIECE: THE LEGION

The heart of the Roman army was the legion, which typically consisted of 4,000 to 6,000 legionaries, heavily armed infantrymen. However, the exact size of the legion could vary, depending on the time period and specific military requirements. Legionaries were equipped with the pilum (a javelin), a gladius (a short sword), a large shield (scutum), armor (lorica segmentata, a type of scale armor) and a helmet. Military service as a legionary offered Roman citizens the opportunity to gain prestige, land and money. Particularly successful legionaries could rise through the ranks and be admitted to the rank of knight (equester) or even senator.

IMMENSE POWER

At the height of the Roman Empire, the standing army usually consisted of between 25 and 30 legions, which amounted to around 100,000 to 180,000 legionaries. In comparison, many of Rome's opponents, such as the various Gallic tribes, Germanic tribes or the Hellenist kingdoms, had much smaller standing armies. These peoples often relied on a combination of warrior aristocracy and militia mobilized in times of crisis. Their armed forces were often less professionalized and not constantly under arms in the same way as the Roman legions.

COHORTS AND CENTURIAS:

Each legion was divided into ten cohorts, and each cohort in turn consisted of six centurias, led by a centurion. The centuria was the basic unit of the Roman army and numbered around 80 to 100 soldiers. A cohort therefore consisted of around 480 to 600 soldiers. The cohort served as the main tactical unit within the legion. In battle, the cohorts acted independently to ensure tactical flexibility. The first cohort of a legion was often larger and better equipped than the others, and could have up to twice as many soldiers. It consisted of the most experienced and bravest legionaries.

THE CENTURION

At the head of a centuria was the centurion, an experienced officer who was chosen for his military skills, leadership qualities and often many years of service. The centurion was a key figure in the Roman army, responsible for the training, discipline and combat leadership of his unit. The name means "leader of a hundred" and refers to the size of the centurias. Centurions often came from the ranks of the legionaries, based on their experience, bravery and leadership ability. Some were promoted based on their performance in battle or by recommendation. However, many of them were simply noblemen who were elevated to such a high position by virtue of their status immediately after their basic training

SUPPORTING ROLE

Each centuria also included non-commissioned officers such as the optio, who acted as the centurion's deputy, and the signifer, who carried the centuria's standard. The standard was a kind of flag or banner and symbolized the unity and fighting spirit of the centurion. It was a focal point for the soldiers and strengthened the feeling of togetherness and pride. On the battlefield, the standard served as a point of orientation for the soldiers, making it easier to find their unit and keep formation. A picture of a standard is also shown later in the book.

CAVALRY (EQUITES)

The Roman legion was not only a collection of infantry units (legionaries), but also included various specialized units that were crucial to the functioning of the army as a whole. One of these units was the equites (the roman knights). They were used for reconnaissance, as a rapid reaction force, to pursue fleeing enemies and to secure the flanks in battle. Although the Roman army already had a clear focus on infantry, cavalry played an important role in tactical warfare.

ROLE OF THE EQUITES

The cavalry was divided into smaller units called turmae, with each turma being led by a decurio. The number of horsemen in a turma could vary, but was typically around 30 to 40 knights. They usually had a lance (hasta) as their primary weapon and a sword in the form of a gladius (short sword) or a spatha (a later, longer sword) as a secondary weapon. Of course, the horse was the most important "equipment" of a cavalryman. Roman cavalry horses were bred for their endurance and reliability, not necessarily for size or speed.

THE ARTILLERY

Heavy weapons were essential for war, with which large groups of enemies, buildings or infrastructure (bridges) could be destroyed. Roman artillery used various weapons, such as ballistae and catapults, which were capable of hurling large projectiles such as stones or arrows over long distances. These weapons were used both in sieges and on open battlefields. Artillery also played a major role in psychological warfare. Enemy soldiers could be quickly intimidated by impressive artillery weapons and their morale and fighting spirit could suffer greatly as a result

TECHNICAL TROOPS

The engineers (fabri) were responsible for the construction of camp fortifications, roads, bridges and siege engines. Their skills were essential for the logistics and mobility of the Roman army. The technical troops also included craftsmen such as blacksmiths, carpenters and metalworkers, who were responsible for the maintenance and repair of equipment and the manufacture of new weapons and devices. The Roman legion can be seen as a small, mobile city that required experts with their own special professions, supplies and social structures.

INFRASTRUCTURE & SUPPLY

In addition to military training, the legionaries were also involved in construction work (such as building camps, roads and fortifications) and agricultural activities to ensure the legion's self-sufficiency. The legions built fortress-like camps (castra), which could become permanent settlements during longer campaigns. These camps had a standardized layout with barracks, command centers, workshops, storehouses and even bathhouses. The latter shows once again how important the luxury of bathing was to the Romans.

LEISURE AND ENTERTAINMENT

The daily life of a legionnaire was characterized by rigorous training, which included both physical fitness and combat skills. This training ensured that the soldiers were prepared for battle and that the discipline of the unit was maintained. Legionnaires also had free time, which they could spend playing games, exercising or visiting baths and canteens, depending on the legion's current location. Faith was not to be neglected either, which is why they had their own altars and shrines for the worship of the Roman gods.

FACTS ABOUT THE LEGIONS
OF THE ROMAN ARMY

The camp design: Roman military camps had a standardized design with rectangular streets, which resembled a checkerboard pattern. This layout facilitated quick mobilization and orientation within the camp.

The lion's heart of a legionnaire: Roman soldiers believed that eating the heart of a strong and courageous animal, such as a lion, would give them courage and strength in battle.

Legionnaires and their personal equipment: A legionnaire had to carry his personal equipment, which could weigh up to 30 kilograms. This concept, known as "Marius' mule", turned the soldiers into their own pack animals.

The Roman tents: In military camps, soldiers lived in tents designed to accommodate eight men. The tents were designed so that they could be dismantled quickly to keep the army mobile.

The ranking of the centurions: There were different ranks of centurions in a legion, and their hierarchy was determined not only by their position in the legion, but also by their position within the formation.

Toilets in military camps: Roman military camps had sophisticated sanitary facilities, including communal toilets that were flushed through an ingenious system of water channels. These sanitary facilities are evidence of advanced Roman engineering.

Birthplace of legionaries: Legionaries were often recruited far away from their birthplace and stationed in other parts of the empire. This encouraged loyalty to the Roman army rather than local ties.

Veterans' settlements: After serving in the army, many veterans received land as part of their pension. This practice encouraged the establishment of settlements in the conquered territories and helped to Romanize these regions.

ROMAN FORMATIONS

Roman formations are probably one of the best-known features of the Roman army. They were the result and implementation of the advanced war strategies of the Roman generals and testified to the tactical superiority of the Romans.

MANIPULAR FORMATION

In the early days of the Republic, the Roman army fought in the manipular formation, which was a more flexible alternative to the rigid phalanx formation (a simple block of spearmen). This formation consisted of three lines: the hastati (young, less experienced soldiers), the principes (in their prime and best equipped) and the triarii (the most experienced and best armed soldiers). This formation made it possible to bring fresh troops into battle while the fighting continued. The manipular formation was often deployed with the support of cavalry and lightly-armed troops (velites). The Velites carried out reconnais sance and disrupted the enemy with thrown weapons before the Hastati launched the first heavy attack. This strategic flexibility made the manipular formation an extremely effective war tactic in antiquity and contributed to Rome's superiority in numerous battles.

TURTLE FORMATION

The testudo formation (turtle formation) was a defensive tactic in which the soldiers held their shields in a roof shape above and in front of them to form a protected block. The Testudo's main strength lay in its ability to provide an almost impenetrable defense against long-range attacks. It was ideal for situations where legionaries were under heavy fire, such as crossing open terrain under enemy fire or storming fortifications. Its greatest weakness was its limited mobility and vulnerability to infantry attacks.

SIEGE WARFARE

The Romans were also masters of siege warfare and developed a variety of machines such as battering rams, siege towers and catapults. Their engineers constructed complex siege works to conquer enemy fortresses. When a direct assault was too risky or difficult, the Romans often resorted to the tactic of starvation, isolating the city and waiting until the defenders surrendered due to lack of food and disease.

STRATEGIC SIEGE

The Roman siege strategy was based on three phases. The first phase was the Reconnaissance. Here the Romans first carried out thorough reconnaissance with scouts to identify weak points in the enemy's defenses. The more information they had, the more effective the next two phases would be. The second phase was the construction of a camp near the place to be besieged. This was followed by the comprehensive siege, the third phase. They often built a complete enclosure around the besieged town or fortress to cut off access to food, water and reinforcements. This included the construction of walls, moats and watchtowers to prevent a breakout and ensure control of the surrounding territory. They also used psychological tactics, such as parading prisoners in front of the walls or offering generous terms of surrender, to break the will of the besieged to resist. Roman siege warfare was characterized by patience, technical innovation and strategic planning. By combining different techniques and the willingness to endure long sieges, they were often able to conquer even well-fortified cities. These strategies ultimately led to the Romans building one of the largest and longest-lasting empires of all time.

MASTER OF DEFENSE

At least as good as their offensive wars was their defense of conquered land. Their ability to secure cities, borders and strategic positions was a key element of their centuries-long military and political dominance.

FORTRESS ARCHITECTURE

Roman cities were often surrounded by mighty walls that were reinforced with towers and gates. These structures were not only physical barriers, but also symbols of power and stability. The walls were often several meters thick and the gates were double, with two sets of doors and a space between them to trap enemies who broke through the first gate. The Romans often pursued a strategy of defense in depth, with several defensive lines laid out behind the border. This gave them time and space to react to invasions and wear down enemy forces. They were never focused on just one fortress, but viewed their entire empire as a defensive system emanating from Rome.

HADRIAN'S WALL

Hadrian's Wall is one of the most impressive structures of the Roman Empire and served as a border defense in Britain. This famous border fortification stretched over 118 kilometers and was intended to secure the northernmost border of Roman Britain. The rampart consisted not only of a stone wall, but was also equipped with a deep ditch, defensive embankments and watchtowers. The rampart was around 3 to 4 meters high and 2 to 3 meters wide, with the exact structure varying in different sections depending on the materials available. Larger fortresses were also built on the rampart, which served as headquarters for the Roman troops and included facilities such as barracks, warehouses, workshops and baths.

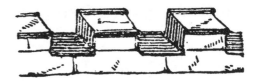

THE ROMAN LIMES

The Roman Limes was an extensive border defense system that secured and monitored the borders of the Roman Empire. The term "limes" comes from the Latin and means "way" or "border". Roads were built along the limes to enable the rapid movement of troops and efficient communication between different points along the border. The Limes itself was a combination of thick walls, ditches, palisades, watchtowers and fortified strongholds.

SLAVES AT WAR

Slaves played an important role in Roman society and were also present in military contexts. In a Roman legion, slaves served in various support functions that were essential for the operation and efficiency of the military unit. However, they usually never took part directly in the fight

PERSONAL SERVANTS

Many officers and high-ranking soldiers had personal slaves known as calones. These served as servants who carried out personal tasks such as washing clothes, preparing meals and looking after equipment. Most people have a false, dirty image of slaves, but Roman slaves were not like that at all. The slaves who served in the Roman army as servants or support roles were, like the soldiers, very disciplined and mostly educated.

SPECIALIZED TASKS

Slaves were used for logistical tasks, such as the transportation of equipment and supplies. They also helped to maintain roads, repair camp facilities and carry out construction work. Some slaves specialized in crafts, such as blacksmithing, carpentry or tailoring, and supported the army by making and repairing equipment and buildings.

BASIC MILITARY TRAINING

Basic military training included physical training, marching exercises, the use of weapons such as the gladius and pilum, as well as formation training and tactical exercises.Depending on their role and unit, soldiers also received special training, e.g. in the operation of siege engines, cavalry combat or other specialized skills.

SERVICE TIME AND CAREER PATH

The regular period of service in the legion was originally 16 years, but was later increased to 20 years and finally to 25 years under Augustus. After their service, veterans often received a pension or land as a reward. With the introduction of the professional army, military service became the main occupation. In addition to their military duties, however, soldiers could also work in the camp workshops, in construction or in other services within the military. The career path of a Roman soldier could start with the position of a simple legionary and lead through various non-commissioned officer ranks such as centurion (commander of a centurion) to higher military positions. Successful soldiers could achieve considerable social advancement and recognition.

CAREER AS A CENTURION

The life of a centurion in the Roman army was characterized by responsibility, discipline and a high degree of social prestige. Centurions usually rose from the ranks of experienced legionaries based on their leadership skills, combat experience and occasionally through political or family connections. A centurion had to be proficient in military skills as well as administrative and leadership duties. Their training included advanced tactics, logistics and personnel management. A centurion was directly responsible for the training, discipline and morale of his centuria. He led his men in battle and ensured that they were well trained and equipped.

RISKS AND REWARDS

The role of a centurion was associated with considerable danger, as they were often on the front line in battle. Their leadership position required courage and a willingness to expose themselves to direct danger. Successful centurions could expect substantial rewards, including financial bonuses, land grants and possibly even political office after their military service.

TRIBUNUS (TRIBUN)

They were directly above the centurions in the hierarchy and were responsible for leading, supervising and evaluating the centurions. Tribunes communicated military orders and strategies to them and ensured that these were properly implemented. Each tribune was assigned a part of a legion, whereby an entire legion usually had 6 tribunes. Even among these 6, however, there was a hierarchy, with the highest-ranking tribune, known as Tribunus Laticlavius, holding a prominent position because he usually came from the senatorial class.

TASK OF THE TRIBUNE

Tribunes were subordinate to the Legatus Legionis, who had overall responsibility for the legion. They carried out the legatus' orders and reported to him on military and administrative matters. Tribunes often came from the Roman aristocracy, especially from senatorial or chivalric (equestrian) families. Many began their career in the army directly as a tribune. Their training as tribunes was not always the same, but they were often trained through direct participation in campaigns or through their role in other military or administrative functions.

THE LEGATUS

The legatus legionis (legatus) was the commanding officer of a legion and usually came from the Roman senatorial class. He was responsible for leading the legion in the field and for strategic decision-making. The tribunes, above all the tribunus laticlavius, were directly subordinate to him. The legate was appointed directly by the emperor (in imperial times) or by the senate (in the Republic). The selection was based on political reliability, military experience and often also on personal relationships with the Roman elite.

STEPPING STONE TO THE TOP

The legatus had a considerable influence on the military strategy and policy of the Roman Empire. His decisions could have far-reaching consequences for the areas in which he operated. Successful service as a legionary legate could form the basis for further advancement in the Roman political hierarchy, up to the highest offices, such as the consulship or a governorship. Caesar, for example, used his position as legatus and his military successes there to gain political power and later become the sole ruler of the Roman Empire.

CLOTHING OF THE LEGIONNAIRES

In the Roman army, ranks were distinguished not only by their functions and responsibilities, but also by their appearance and equipment. Legionaries wore a fairly uniform outfit consisting of a tunic, armor (usually the well-known lorica segmentata, an armor made of metal strips), a helmet (galea), a large shield (scutum) and military insignia that indicated their rank, unit and function. This allowed them to be immediately recognized and assigned by other soldiers or their generals.

CLOTHING OF THE CENTURIONS

Centurions wore the visually striking helmet with a transverse crest (crista transversa), which indicated their position. Their tunic could also be richer and more colorful. Centurions often carried a vine (vitis) as a sign of their authority and wore special armor that emphasized their position and experience.

CLOTHING OF THE TRIBUNES

As officers of higher social rank, tribunes often wore richer and flashier clothing and armor. Their tunics and cloaks (paludamentum) were often made of finer material and bright colors. Tribunes wore special insignia that marked their position and rank and their helmets could have additional extravagant decorations. In general, everything about them appeared more valuable than that of centurions or ordinary legionaries. From this rank upwards, individuality was also very important. Their armor and cloaks were all personally tailored to them and had special features that corresponded to their preferences.

CLOTHING OF THE LEGATUS

The legatus, differed again clearly in hisappearance. They often wore a special tunic that was richer and more colorful than that of ordinary soldiers. Over their tunic they wore a paludamentum, a cloak-like cloak that was typically dyed purple, a color that symbolized power and authority in Rome. A legate's armour was of high quality and could be adorned with silver, gold or other decorations to emphasize his high rank and importance. The armor was not only functional, but also a status symbol.

WAR AT SEA

The conflict in the First Punic War with Carthage (~264 BC), an established naval power with a strong navy, forced Rome to rethink its naval strategy and build up its own fleet. Rome was already a nation of experienced infantrymen, but they had little experience in naval battles. It began building large warships, in particular quinque-remen, modeled after the design of captured Carthaginian ships. This marked the beginning of Roman naval power.

INNOVATION OF SEA BATTLES

One of the most important innovations for the Romans was the development of the corvus, a boarding bridge that enabled Roman soldiers to board enemy ships. This advantage enabled the Romans to compensate for their weakness and inexperience in naval battles and force their enemies into close combat. The Romans were therefore aware of their weaknesses and tried to use this strategy to make naval battles more like land battles, as their soldiers were superior to most of their enemies, especially in man-to-man combat.

CORVUS

The Corvus was basically a large, movable boarding bridge mounted on the deck of a ship. It consisted of a long, narrow wooden walkway attached to a rotating joint, which allowed a certain amount of maneuverability in different directions. At the tip of the corvus was a heavy, iron grappling hook designed to claw into the decks of enemy ships. As soon as the hook caught an enemy ship, the bar could be locked to create a stable connection between the two ships.

BOARDING

Until the development of the Corvus, boarding was not a common strategy of warfare at sea. Most naval powers used projectiles or rammed their enemies. They preferred to keep their distance and avoided close combat to minimize losses. It was the Romans' courage and awareness of their strengths and weaknesses that led to the development of this new strategy.

THE TRIREMES

The triremes (ships with three rows of oars) were one of the most common types of ship in the Roman navy. They were mainly used for fast attacks, reconnaissance and patrols. Their speed and maneuverability made them ideal ships for hit-and-run tactics and naval blockades. On board was a crew of around 170 to 200 men, including oarsmen, soldiers and sailors. The oarsmen were arranged in three tiers one above the other and worked in perfect coordination to move the ship. The ships were usually between 30 and 40 meters long.

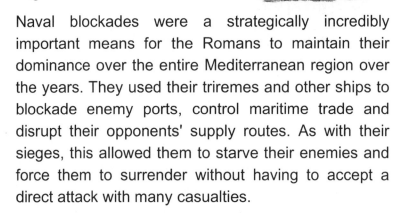

NAVAL BLOCKADES

Naval blockades were a strategically incredibly important means for the Romans to maintain their dominance over the entire Mediterranean region over the years. They used their triremes and other ships to blockade enemy ports, control maritime trade and disrupt their opponents' supply routes. As with their sieges, this allowed them to starve their enemies and force them to surrender without having to accept a direct attack with many casualties.

QUINQUEREMEN

Quinqueremen were larger and more robust than triremes and had five oarsmen per row of oars. These ships were around 45 to 50 meters long. They could accommodate up to 300 oarsmen plus soldiers and sailors, which meant that the total crew often amounted to over 400 men. Due to their size and strength, quinqueremen were better suited for main battles at sea. In addition to the ramming spur, the traditional main weapon of ancient warships, they could also carry more soldiers and siege equipment such as catapults and were therefore crucial for major conflicts and naval battles. The ships also had reinforced hulls to enable the use of the corvus and the associated loads.

SUPPLIES AND REPAIRS

Logistical support and the ability to repair were critical elements in Roman naval warfare that determined the operational success of their navy. We have already seen how organizationally and strategically adept the Romans were, and this is exactly what they demonstrated in naval warfare. They often spent several weeks or months at a time at sea, which made a functioning supply and repairs after a battle essential

SUPPLY

Supplying sufficient food and drinking water was a major challenge, especially on longer voyages. The Romans organized extensive supply chains to provide their ships with necessary supplies such as grain, olive oil, wine and salted meat. The fleet needed a continuous supply of weapons, arrows and other military equipment. These goods were stored in larger naval bases and distributed to the ships as required. The Romans developed special supply ships for these tasks, which were used to transport food, fresh water and other supplies to the warships. Without this infrastructure and meticulous planning, it would never have been possible to carry out months-long naval battles and sieges.

REPAIR FACILITIES

Large Roman ports such as Ostia or Misenum were equipped with shipyards and dry docks where ships could be repaired and maintained. These facilities were crucial for maintaining the strength of the fleet. In some cases, mobile repair facilities were used to repair the ships directly at the places where they were used. This enabled the Roman fleet to maintain its operational capability away from the main bases. These were housed on special ships and served as floating workshops.

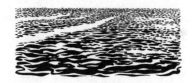

EXPANSION OF SEA POWER

Emperor Augustus recognized the importance of naval power for securing the empire and protecting the extensive coastal areas of the Mediterranean.He made great efforts to develop the Roman navy into a professional and well-organized force.He founded the two largest fleets in the empire, the Classis Misenensis, stationed in Misenum near Naples, and the Classis Ravennatis, stationed in Ravenna on the Adriatic coast.These fleets served as the core of Rome's sea-based defense strategy.

PEAK OF POWER

The exact size of the Roman fleet varies according to source and date, but at its peak it may have totaled over 400 ships, including large warships such as quinquerems as well as numerous smaller ships and auxiliary units. The Roman fleet was not only present in the Mediterranean, but also conducted operations in the Black Sea, the Atlantic and the estuaries of the Rhine and Danube, making it a global power presence.

FUNCTIONS AND ROLES

After Rome had controlled almost everything in the Mediterranean, the focus of the fleet shifted more to defensive functions. The main tasks of the Roman navy included fighting piracy, protecting trade routes, securing Roman rule over the provinces and supporting battles at ports that were fought simultaneously on land and at sea. In addition to its military role, the Roman navy was also crucial for the logistical support of the Roman army, transporting troops, food and equipment over long distances. Despite the many successes and military might of the Roman navy, the focus of the empire remained on its original strength, namely land battles with its legions.

FACTS ABOUT THE MARITIME POWER OF THE ROMAN EMPIRE

Oarsmen without oars: It is reported that in the early days of their navy, the Romans forgot the rowing benches on some ships when building their first fleet because they simply did not know how to construct a ship properly.

Quick end to the pirates: The famous Roman general Pompey was given the task of fighting piracy in the Mediterranean. He managed to completely destroy them in just 3 months, which was another display of Roman dominance.

Luxury on the flagship: Caligula, who was known for his extravagances, is said to have owned a floating palace galley with marble floors, golden taps and even a heated swimming pool.

THE HISTORY OF THE
ROMAN EMPIRE

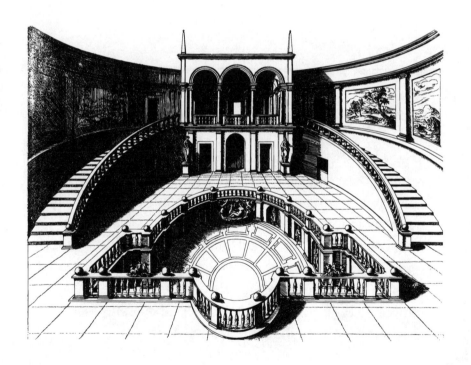

THE WHOLE STORY

The early Roman Empire saw the light of day in 753 BC and existed for over 700 years, until the 5th century AD. It was the largest and longest-lived empire the world had ever seen. The period of the Roman Empire can be divided into 3 major phases:

1. the Roman Kingdom (ca. 753-509 BC)
2. the Roman Republic (509-27 BC)
3. the Roman Empire (27 BC to 476 AD)

THE WESTERN ROMAN EMPIRE

The Western Roman Empire ended in 476 AD with the deposition of the last Western Roman emperor Romulus Augustulus, who was named after the mythological founder of Rome. One could therefore poetically claim that the Roman Empire began and ended with a Romulus. However, the Eastern Roman Empire, also known as the Byzantine Empire, lasted almost 1,000 years longer, until the conquest of Constantinople by the Ottomans in 1453 AD.

MYTHS ABOUT FOUNDERS

A fascinating legend about the founding of Rome is the story of Romulus and Remus. According to myth, they were the twin sons of Mars, the god of war, and Rhea Silvia, the priestess. As adults, Romulus and Remus decided to found a city on the site of their rescue (more on this in a moment). However, a dispute over the location and name of the city led to Romulus killing his brother Remus and naming the city after himself (Rome). This event is traditionally dated to 753 BC and marks the beginning of Roman history.

FAMILY CONFLICT

According to Roman mythology, Romulus and Remus were the grandsons of Numitor, the rightful king of Alba Longa, a city near what would later become Rome. Their uncle Amulius had dethroned their grandfather in order to gain control himself and wanted to ensure that Numitor's descendants, Romulus and Remus, could not lay claim to the throne of Alba Longa. To thwart their possible claims to power, they were abandoned as babies in a basket on the Tiber. The Tiber is the third longest Italian river and flows through Rome.

RAISED BY WOLVES

The legend goes on to say that the two infants were found and suckled by a she-wolf by the river, an image that became an iconic symbol of Rome as the "Capitoline Wolf". The brothers were later found and raised by a shepherd.

THE CAPITOLINE WOLF

The Capitoline Wolf (lat. Lupa Capitolina) is a life-size bronze figure of a she-wolf suckling Romulus and Remus. The sculpture is 75 cm high and 114 cm wide and is located in the Capitoline Museums in Rome. It is said to date back to the 5th century BC, but doubts have recently been raised as the techniques used were unknown before the 11th century AD. Today it is estimated that the figure was made in the Middle Ages between the 9th and 13th centuries.

THE FIRST KING OF ROME

After Romulus founded Rome, legend has it that he became the first king of Rome and thus the first ruler of the Roman Empire. Apart from myths, not much is known about this period.

Romulus is said to have ruled Rome and established various social and political institutions, including the Senate, which consisted of the oldest and wisest men in the community.

In order to increase Rome's population, Romulus is said to have introduced the right of asylum, whereby refugees and outcasts from other areas found refuge in Rome. However, this led to an imbalance between men and women, which Romulus resolved by abducting women from the neighboring Sabine people, an event known as "The Rape of the Sabine Women".

After this conflict, peace was made through the mediation of the Sabine abductees, with the Sabine king Titus Tatius ruling Rome together with Romulus for a time.

THE DEATH OF ROMULUS

Romulus is said to have mysteriously disappeared. According to Roman legends, he was elevated to the status of a god. After his disappearance, other kings followed, among whom Numa Pompilius is known as the second king of Rome. Although his historical existence has not been clearly proven, he has a firm place in Roman culture as a wise and pious ruler who became famous for his religious reforms.

THE ROMAN KINGDOM

Between 753 and 509 BC, various kings ruled over the Roman Empire. Rome was therefore a monarchy during this period. However, unlike in most monarchies, the crown was not awarded on the basis of blood relationship, but was determined by the people and the religious community through complicated processes. This reflected the Roman belief that political leadership should be based on both the will of the people and the approval of the gods. It also shows how political, religious and social elements were intertwined in Rome.

FACTS ABOUT
THE KINGDOM

Military strength: Rome had developed a strong military presence and was able to subdue several local tribes and cities, consolidating its position of power in the region of Latium.

Urban development: Rome had developed from a small settlement on the Tiber into an urban center with various districts, public buildings, temples and a forum.

Population growth: Estimates of the size of the population vary, but by the end of the Romen Kingdom could have had between 35,000 and 100,000 inhabitants, which was considered huge by the standards of the time.

The kings: There were a total of 7 kings in the Romen Kingdom, beginning with Romulus and ending with Lucius Tarquinius Superbus, who was considered a tyrant and overthrown.

ORIGIN OF THE REVOLUTION

The reign of the last king, Lucius Tarquinius Superbus (ruled from 535 to 509 BC), was characterized by his tyrannical rule and abuse of power. His rule and the abuses under his leadership led to considerable discontent among the Roman citizens.

THE FALL OF THE MONARCHY

According to legend, the immediate cause of the fall of the monarchy was the rape of Lucretia, a Roman noblewoman, by Sextus Tarquinius, the king's son. This crime and Lucretia's subsequent suicide triggered a wave of outrage, led by Lucius Junius Brutus, a relative of the king.

Brutus called on the Romans to put an end to royal rule and establish a new form of government. The population rose up against Tarquinius Superbus, who was subsequently expelled from Rome.

FOUNDING OF THE REPUBLIC

After the expulsion of the last king, the Romans ushered in a new era by founding the Republic. The transition to a republic was not an immediate or completely smooth process. There were several attempts to regain power, and in the following years the new republican system had to consolidate and stabilize.

MULTIPLE LEADERS

Instead of a single king, there were two consuls who were elected each year. This ensured that power was divided and neither could become too powerful.

TERM LIMITS

Each consul was only allowed to hold office for one year and could not be immediately re-elected. This regulation prevented the long-term accumulation of power in one person.

SENATE AS AN ADVISORY BODY

The Senate, consisting of experienced statesmen, played a central role in politics. It advised the consuls and had great influence on decisions, which ensured stability and continuity.

PEOPLE'S TRIBUNES TO PROTECT THE CITIZENS

The introduction of tribunes of the people, who were specifically supposed to represent the interests of the common people (plebeians), strengthened the democratic elements. These tribunes had the power to block laws and decisions of the consuls if they appeared unfair.

REGULATIONS FOR FAIR DECISION-MAKING

The establishment of various offices and assemblies ensured that many citizens were involved in the decision-making processes and were able to have their say in the election of the leadership and changes to the law.

PREVENTING ABUSE OF POWER

The focus of the Roman Republic's system of government was clearly to prevent abuse of power at all costs. It aimed to achieve this by involving the most diverse social classes in political processes and decisions. This idea formed the foundation of the next 500 years of the Roman Republic.

ESTATES BATTLES

Over a period of almost 200 years, internal conflicts took place between the patricians (the nobility) and the plebeians (the commoners). These struggles between the estates were mainly driven by social and economic inequalities. The patricians had access to most political offices and controlled the Senate, while the plebeians, who made up most of the population and the army, had little political influence and were often economically disadvantaged. It is easiest to compare it with today's gap between rich and poor, although it was much more complex than just the purely financial aspect. Thanks to the political foundation of the Republic and the tenacity of the plebeians, several political achievements and reforms were made over time.

POLITICAL INTEGRATION

Through the struggles between the estates, the plebeians were gradually more integrated into the Roman political system, which led to a more balanced distribution of power. It also opened up paths to political power and social advancement for the plebeians, despite social and economic differences.

THE CONQUEST OF ITALY

Between 343 and 264 BC in particular, Rome waged a series of wars against other Italian tribes and cities, known as the Samnite Wars, and other local conflicts that eventually led to Roman domination of Italy.

WHY IT WAS SO IMPORTANT TO CONTROL ITALY

These conquests transformed Rome from a city-state into a powerful republic that controlled the entire Italian peninsula. This expansion laid the foundations for Rome's subsequent rise to become the dominant power in the entire Mediterranean region. The conquest of Italy was also decisive for the development of the Roman military, economy and infrastructure, as Rome gained access to important resources, new trade routes and strategic military bases through these conquests.

THE PUNIC WARS

The Punic Wars were a series of three conflicts between Rome and Carthage that lasted from 264 to 146 BC. They are among the most important wars in ancient history and had a decisive impact on the balance of power in the western Mediterranean.

THE FIRST PUNIC WAR

The war began because of the competition for control of Sicily. Both powers, Rome and Carthage, wanted to expand their spheres of influence, which led to tensions and ultimately to war. The war was mainly fought at sea and in Sicily. Rome built its first large fleet at this time in order to compete with Carthage's superior navy. This turned out to be a great success, as Rome won the war and made Sicily the first Roman provincial territory outside Italy.

THE SECOND PUNIC WAR

The most famous Punic War and generally one of the most famous wars in history, primarily because of the Carthaginian general Hannibal Barkas, who crossed the Alps with elephants to attack Rome directly. Hannibal went on to lead successful campaigns in Italy, including victory at the Battle of Cannae (216 BC). However, he was unable to defeat Rome decisively. Rome recovered from the initial defeats, took the fight to North Africa and defeated Carthage at the Battle of Zama (202 BC). The war ended with a Roman victory and Carthage lost its position of power in the Mediterranean.

ELEPHANTS IN THE ALPS

Today it is unthinkable that elephants once roamed the Alps. Although they did not live there, Hannibal led an army of elephants across the Alps to attack Rome directly. The elephants were actually inefficient in direct combat, but they could carry huge amounts of weight and made a menacing impression. This was intended to frighten the Roman soldiers and weaken their morale. How Hannibal managed to bring the elephants across the Alps is still unclear today.

THE THIRD PUNIC WAR

Despite Carthage's weakened position, Rome's fear of a renewed Carthaginian threat remained. Rome finally looked for a pretext to destroy Carthage once and for all and attack again. Rome laid siege to Carthage, which defended itself desperately but was ultimately defeated by the Roman forces. Carthage was then completely destroyed by the Romans in 146 BC, its population was killed or sold into slavery and the city was razed to the ground. The city of Carthage itself was located in North Africa, near modern-day Tunis in Tunisia. The last territories of Carthage now also became Roman provinces.

EXPANSION INTO THE MEDITERRANEAN REGION

After this historic and cruel victory over Carthage, Rome expanded its territories into the eastern Mediterranean, including Greece, Asia Minor, Syria and Egypt.

GAIUS JULIUS CAESAR

Now we come to the end of the Roman Republic, and thus also to the most important figure of this period: Gaius Iulius Caesa (Gaius Julius Caesar).

Caeser was born exactly in the year 100 BC. By Roman standards, he did not come from a wealthy family. Like many rulers of Ancient Rome, however, his origins are surrounded by many myths. For example, his roots can be traced back to Iulus, the son of the Trojan prince Aeneas, who, according to legend, was the son of the goddess Venus. At the height of his power in 45 BC, Caesar had a temple built in honour of Venus to emphasize his connection to this goddess.

FACTS ABOUT
JULIUS CAESAR

Caesar was kidnapped by pirates as a young man. He is said to have told his captors that he would return after his release and crucify them all - a promise he actually kept after his release.

First name Julius, not Caesar: "Caesar" was actually his family name. Julius was his first name, and he was usually called Gaius Julius Caesar.

The month of July (lat. Julius) was named after Julius Caesar to honor his introduction of the Julian calendar.

Vegan salad? Despite the popular legend, Caesar salad has nothing to do with Julius Caesar. It was invented by an Italian-American chef called Caesar Cardini.

Contrary to the belief of many that Caesar came to power through military prowess alone, his rise began in traditional Roman politics. He held offices within the Roman Republic, including quaestor, aedile, pontifex maximus and finally consul in 59 BC. He therefore had a very linear career path. Through great perseverance, he became consul at the age of 41. At the height of his power, Caesar was 64.

OFFICE AS QUAESTOR

A quaestor was a lower office holder in the Roman Republic and later in the Roman Empire, who was mainly entrusted with financial and administrative tasks.

OFFICE AS AEDILE

In his office as aedile, Caesar supervised public order, municipal facilities and the organization of public games and festivals.

OFFICE AS PONTIFEX MAXIMUS

The Pontifex Maximus was the highest religious office in ancient Rome, a title that can be translated as "supreme bridge-builder". This title symbolically reflects the role of the Pontifex Maximus as a mediator between the gods and the people.

THE CONQUEST OF GAUL

After his office as consul, Caesar carried out the conquest of Gaul as proconsul from 58 to 50 BC, which brought him considerable wealth and military power.

CAESAR WANTED MORE

After Julius Caesar had conquered Gaul, he continued his ambitions to gain central political power in Rome. As his political opponents, in particular Pompey Magnus, feared that Caesar could become too powerful too quickly, they manipulated the Roman Senate. The latter then asked Caesar to resign his command and return to Rome as a private citizen. Caesar sought a second term as consul without resigning his military command in Gaul, which was incompatible with Roman law and served as justification for the Senate's demand.

THE RUBICON AND CIVIL WAR

At the beginning of 49 BC, Caesar made a momentous decision: he crossed the Rubicon River, the border between his province and Italy, with a legion and the famous exclamation "Alea iacta est" ("The die is cast"). This act was a direct declaration of war to the Senate and in particular to Pompey. The ensuing civil war between the Caesarians and the Pompeians (supporters of the Senate and Pompey) led Caesar across the Roman Empire, from Italy to Greece, Egypt, North Africa and back to Spain.

SOLE SOVEREIGN

After Ceaser had defeated his enemies following a series of military conflicts, he was appointed dictator for life in 46 BC, making him the sole and most powerful ruler of the Roman Empire. However, the concentration of power caused mistrust, fear and dissatisfaction among many Romans.

CAESAR'S POPULARITY

As a dictator, he benefited from the fact that he was generally very popular with the Roman population. Thanks to his many conquests, he was able to distribute a great deal of wealth among the citizens. He organized games and public celebrations, built public buildings and distributed land to poor citizens, which further increased his popularity.

POLITICAL REFORMS

As dictator, Caesar carried out a series of reforms that improved the lives of the urban and agricultural population. These included the reorganization of debts, improvements to the calendar (introduction of the Julian calendar) and the extension of civil rights to many provincial inhabitants.

CHARISM

Like many political leaders or dictators, Caesar was known for his charisma and rhetorical skills. He was able to inspire and convince people with his oratory skills, which secured him the support and loyalty of broad sections of the population.

MURDER

Due to Caesar's great monopoly on power and personal rivalry in the Senate, a conspiracy was formed against Caesar with the aim of assassinating him. On March 15, 44 BC, he was murdered in the Senate building, the Pompey Theater. The conspirators, around 60 senators, lured him into a meeting and attacked him with daggers. Caesar was killed with 23 stab wounds, which shows that the assassination was carried out by several to share responsibility among the conspirators. Among the conspirators and one of their leaders was Marcus Junius Brutus, who had a special relationship with Caesar.

CAESAR'S LAST WORDS

Caesar's famous last words "Et tu, Brute?" ("You too, Brutus?") are literary and come from Shakespeare's drama "Julius Caesar". In historical accounts, his last words are less clear; some sources claim he said nothing, while others report that he said in Greek "καὶ σύ, τέκνον;" ("You too, my child?") when he saw Brutus among the attackers.

A SECRET SON?

For no known reason, Caesar supported Brutus throughout his political career. Although Brutus fought on the side of Caesar's political opponents during the civil war, Caesar forgave him and paved the way for Brutus to enter the Senate and Caesar also gave him other offices and honors. There have been rumors (though not historically confirmed) that he may have been Brutus' biological father, based on his relationship with Brutus' mother, Servilia. This would explain why Caesar trusted Brutus, why he supported him politically despite his betrayal, and why he was surprised in the end to see Brutus among the conspirators.

VACUUM OF POWER

After Caesar's death, many things became more complicated. The resulting power vacuum attracted many people who wanted to rule Rome. Although he named Octavian (later known as Augustus) as his heir and successor in his will, the political situation was initially unclear and controversial. There was another civil war and many problems until things finally improved.

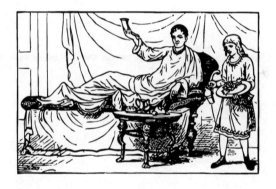

THE ROMAN EMPIRE

The Battle of Actium in 31 BC, in which Octavian decisively defeated Marcus Antonius and Cleopatra, marked the end of the civil wars and the beginning of a new era. In 27 BC, Octavian, now called Augustus, initiated a series of reforms that formally ended the Roman Republic for good and established the Roman Empire, with Augustus as the first emperor.

CLEOPATRA

Everyone knows the name Cleopatra, but few know her history or her political influence in ancient times. She was the last active ruler of Ptolemaic Egypt, a Greek/Macedonian dynasty that ruled Egypt after the death of Alexander the Great. She is one of the most famous figures in ancient history, renowned for her intelligence and political skill.

DEADLY LOVE

After an internal power struggle, Cleopatra fled Egypt, but returned with the support of Julius Caesar, with whom she entered into a love affair. This alliance helped her to consolidate her power over Egypt. After Caesar's assassination, Cleopatra became closely linked to Marcus Antonius, one of the leading Romans after Caesar. Their relationship led to a political alliance that strengthened both their power, but also intensified the political conflict with Octavian (Augustus). Octavian saw their relationship as a threat to Rome, which led to war between the two powers. In the end, Cleopatra took her own life in 30 BC to avoid imprisonment and a life of humiliation.

FACTS ABOUT
CLEOPATRA

Not Egyptian: Despite the close historical connection, Cleopatra was not Egyptian, but belonged to the Ptolemaic dynasty, which only ruled Egypt for a time.

Linguistic talent: Cleopatra was known to have mastered many languages, allegedly around nine - she was also the first of her dynasty to learn Egyptian, the language of the local population.

Innovative cosmetics: Cleopatra was known for her beauty care and is said to have developed many cosmetic products herself.

Cleopatra's Needles: "Cleopatra's Needles" are two Egyptian obelisks located in London and New York. Despite their name, they have nothing directly to do with Cleopatra, as they were erected around 1,500 years before her time.

GAIUS OCTAVIUS

Gaius Octavius was the posthumously adopted great-nephew and heir of Julius Caesar. After Caesar's death in 44 BC, Octavian began to shape his political and military career. After Caesar's death, Octavian returned to Rome to take up his inheritance. Despite his youth and relative inexperience, he garnered support and power by winning over Caesar's veterans and staking his claim to the inheritance. After defeating Marcus Antonius and Cleopatra at the Battle of Actium in 31 BC, Octavian became the undisputed ruler of Rome.

THE EMPEROR AUGUSTUS

In 27 BC, Octavian officially assumed the title "Augustus", which means "the exalted" or "the venerable". This marked the beginning of his official reign as the first Roman emperor. Augustus never called himself emperor, but "Princeps Senatus" (First of the Senate) to emphasize the republican character of his government. This designation characterized his role as first among equals and not as a monarchical ruler.

REIGN OF AUGUSTUS

Augustus reformed the political system in order to centralize power while maintaining the appearance of republican traditions. He retained the title "Princeps", meaning "the first" or "leading citizen", and avoided the active designation "king" or "emperor". He restored the Senate, reduced its membership and concentrated decision-making power in his hands in order to increase the efficiency and stability of the government. Augustus invested heavily in the infrastructure of Rome and the provinces, including the construction of roads, temples, theaters and aqueducts. Under his rule, Rome was literally transformed into a city of marble.

PAX ROMANA

The "Pax Romana", which means "Roman peace", began under his rule. Although the empire expanded enormously as a result of Augustus' military operations, his focus was also on securing the borders and ensuring stability within the empire. The Pax Romana thus began with Augustus and lasted for around 200 years, from 27 BC to around 180 AD. It then ended with the death of Emperor Marcus Aurelius.

CULTURAL CHANGE

The Augustan era saw a flourishing of the arts and literature, supported by Augustus and his advisors. Poets such as Virgil, Horace and Ovid were among the literary greats of this period. Augustus promoted traditional Roman moral values and institutions through laws on marriage, family and public morality. He also restored ancient religious cults and temples and combined his rule with religious authority, often portraying himself as a semi-divine figure.

DIPLOMACY AND THE MILITARY

Overall, Augustus expanded the borders of his empire enormously. However, one of his most important tools besides warfare was diplomacy. For example, he successfully expanded into the East by stabilizing relations with the Parthians (in present-day Iran), which led to the return of standards that had been lost in earlier conflicts. This was a significant diplomatic success.

STANDART

Standards, often referred to as "signa" in the Roman context or specifically for legions as "aquilae" (eagles), were flags or banners that served as military symbols. They were not only a mark of the Roman army, but also a sign of the honor and pride of a unit. They were more than just physical objects; they were central symbols of Roman military and cultural tradition, embodying power, faith and identity within the Roman Empire. The loss of a standard was considered a great dishonor and could damage the honor of the military unit concerned. Its recovery was therefore of great importance.

STANDARD OF THE PARTHIANS

The return of the standards by the Parthians was a significant event, as they had been captured in earlier conflicts, particularly after the Battle of Carrhae in 53 BC. The loss of these standards was a severe blow to Roman prestige. The recovery of these was a great success and thus underlined Augustus' qualities as a leader.

FACTS ABOUT EMPEROR AUGUSTUS

Book censorship: Augustus burned around 2,000 scrolls that he considered inappropriate or dangerous for Roman morals, while at the same time promoting literature that strengthened the spirit of his regime.

Fear of lightning: Augustus suffered from an extreme fear of lightning and thunder. He is said to have hidden during thunderstorms, sometimes under a bed, for fear of being struck by lightning.

Minimalism: Augustus was known for his modest lifestyle. He preferred simple clothing and meals and lived in a relatively inconspicuous house compared to the residences of many of his contemporaries and successors.

The alleged last words: It is reported that Augustus jokingly asked on his deathbed whether he had performed well in the role of his life and asked those present to applaud as if the curtain was falling on a play.

FROM AUGUSTUS TO NERO

Augustus reigned from 27 BC until his death in 14 AD. Augustus ruled for a full 41 years, making him the longest ruler of the Roman Empire of all time. After Augustus, Emperor Tiberius ruled from 14 to 37 AD, Emperor Caligula from 37 to 41 AD and Emperor Claudius from 41 to 54 AD. Claudius, who conquered Britain during his reign and thus drastically expanded the Roman Empire once again, was followed by the famous Emperor Nero from 54 to 68 AD.

YOUNG EMPEROR

Nero's mother Agrippina was the daughter of Emperor Claudius' brother. She later married her uncle (Emperor Claudius), thereby securing Nero as heir to the empire. Nero then became emperor at the age of 16 after Claudius died in 54 AD, with Agrippina playing a crucial role in his ascension to the throne and rumors say that she may have contributed to Claudius' death. Especially in the early years, Nero was supported by many advisors and was considered a very innovative and moderate ruler.

THE GREAT FIRE OF ROME

Almost the entire city burned for 6 days and 7 nights. Of the 14 districts of Rome, 3 were completely destroyed and 7 were severely damaged. It is considered one of the greatest disasters of antiquity. The exact cause of the fire is unknown, but due to the way Rome was built, with narrow streets and mainly wooden structures, the fire spread quickly.

NERO THE ARSONIST?

Emperor Nero was accused by some contemporaries and later historians of having either started the fire or at least exploited it. Nero was in his villa in Antium (now Anzio) during the fire and returned to Rome to extinguish it. There is still no evidence or connection between the fire and Nero, but Nero used the fire for personal gain.

UTILIZATION OF THE FIRE

Nero used the destruction of the fire to build a new palace complex, the Domus Aurea. Today, the Domus Aurea is a much-visited site and a tourist attraction in Rome.

THE CHRISTIANS WERE BLAMED

In order to refute the rumors that accused him of causing the fire, Nero is said to have used the Christians as scapegoats, which led to one of the first major persecutions of this religious group in the Roman Empire. Nero thus went down in history as one of the greatest persecutors of Christians of all time.

REBUILDING

After the fire, the houses were rebuilt to be much more fireproof. Nero ordered wider streets and changed the cityscape considerably. On the one hand, to make it safer from another fire, but also to rebuild the city more aesthetically pleasing in his eyes. Nero was a fanatic of the arts, who often performed in theaters himself and was celebrated for it. He took every opportunity, including the great fire, to reshape and beautify the city according to his vision. Part of the area affected by the fire was used for the construction of Nero's opulent palace complex, the Domus Aurea. This move, as well as Nero's behavior during and after the fire, contributed to his bad reputation.

DECLINE OF NERO

Nero increasingly lost the support of the Senate, the military and the people. His decline led to a rebellion in 68 AD, which forced him to step down from power. After being declared an enemy of the state, Nero committed suicide on June 9, 68 AD, ushering in the Year of the Four Emperors, a period of civil wars and political instability.

YEAR OF THE FOUR EMPERORS

Galba, Otho, Vitellius and finally Vespasian all ruled the Roman Empire in succession as emperor in 69 AD. All four defeated their respective predecessors through military might. This showed the weakness of the political system and the growing power of the military. Whoever had the loyalty of the legions behind them became the decisive factor in determining who became emperor. The final seizure of power by Vespasian ended this year of civil war in December and he ruled as emperor for another 10 years.

EMPEROR TITUS

Emperor Titus was Vespasian's successor and completed the construction of the Colosseum, which Vespasian had begun. He reigned at the time of the eruption of Mount Vesuvius, which destroyed Pompeii and Herculaneum.

POMPEJI

Pompeii had an estimated population of around 10,000 to 20,000 people. The population was a mixture of Romans, Italians, Greeks, Jews and other groups, which made the city very culturally diverse. The eruption of Mount Vesuvius came as a surprise and covered the city with a thick layer of ash and pumice in a flash. The buried city was only rediscovered in the 18th century. Excavations revealed an exceptionally well-preserved snapshot of Roman life, as the rapid burial under the ash resulted in remarkable preservation of buildings, objects and even body casts. The remains of Pompeii are now one of the most important and famous archaeological sites in the world.

THE FIVE GOOD EMPERORS

Titus was followed by Domitian, whose reign ultimately ended with his assassination. He was followed by Nerva, Trajan, Hadrian, Antoninus Pius and Marcus Aurelius, who are known as the "five good emperors". They became famous for their competent and relatively peaceful rule. They ruled successively from 96 to 180 AD and are regarded as examples of effective and stable governance.

THE HEIGHT OF THE ROMAN EMPIRE

The period of the five good emperors is often seen as the high point of the Roman Empire. With Trajan, the second of the Five Good Emperors, who ruled from 98 to 117 AD, the empire grew to its maximum size. He conquered Eastern Europe, the Middle East and North Africa without causing political or cultural instability within the country. The economy and Roman culture flourished during this time. The Roman Empire was bigger, richer and more powerful than ever before.

MARCUS AURELIUS

Marcus Aurelius ruled from 161 to 180 AD, initially together with his adoptive brother Lucius Verus until the latter's death in 169 AD. This was one of the few times in Roman history when there were two emperors with equal rights. Marcus Aurelius ruled during a very difficult period characterized by wars and the plague. The latter wiped out a considerable part of the population, which led to many other problems. Despite these circumstances, Marcus Aurelius managed to stabilize the people and go down in Roman history as one of the wisest and most successful rulers.

STOIC PHILOSOPHY

Marcus Aurelius is often portrayed as a "philosopher emperor", a ruler who strove to exercise his power wisely and justly, following the principles of reason and morality. He is considered the most important philosopher of Stoic philosophy. His work "Mediations" ("Ta eis heauton", literally "[things] for themselves") in particular shaped Stoicism and is still one of the best-selling philosophy books in the world today. Stoicism simply explained is a philosophy of life that states that we should live virtuously and in harmony with rationality and nature.

BASIC STOIC CONSIDERATIONS

Only control what you can: Distinguish between things you can control and those that are out of your control.

Accept the inevitable: Learn to accept the inevitable and not get angry about situations you can't change.

Live in harmony with nature: Act according to your nature as a rational and social being. This means living ethically, working for the common good and using your reason to lead a virtuous life.

Practice gratitude and humility: Practice gratitude for what you have and avoid excessive desire for more.

END OF THE PAX ROMANA

Marcus Aurelius died in 180 AD in Vindobona (modern-day Vienna) during a campaign. His death marked the end of the Pax Romana and the beginning of a period of major military and political challenges for the Roman Empire.

THOSE WHO FLY HIGH, FALL DEEP

Marcus Aurelius' son, Commodus, succeeded him. Due to his mismanagement and increasing autocracy, this period is considered the beginning of the decline of the Roman Empire. The assassination of Commodus was followed by a short, turbulent period that ultimately led to the establishment of the Severan dynasty, beginning with Septimius Severus. This period was characterized by military expansion and a strengthening of the army, but also by financial problems. It was one of the last rallies of the Roman Empire before it fell on hard times.

THE CRISIS OF THE 3RD CENTURY

The 3rd century was a period of extreme instability. This period was characterized by frequent changes of emperor, civil wars, economic difficulties, plague epidemics and threats from external enemies such as the Germanic tribes and the Sassanids.

CONSTANTINE THE GREAT

Constantine the Great, also known as Constantine I, was one of the most important emperors of the Roman Empire. His reign from 306 to 337 AD marked a turning point in Roman history, in particular through the promotion of Christianity and the founding of Constantinople as the new capital.

FOUNDATION OF CONSTANTINOPLE

Constantine founded the city of Constantinople (now Istanbul) on the site of the old Byzantium and made it the new capital of the Roman Empire. Constantinople was conceived as a Christian city and was to become the center of imperial power and Christianity. The reason for Constantinople as the new capital had several strategic, economic and political reasons. The city was naturally well defended, surrounded by water on three sides and easy to fortify. These natural advantages offered protection against invasions.

FAR AWAY FROM ROME

Rome was deeply rooted in tradition and characterized by political intrigue. Constantinople offered the opportunity to establish a new administrative structure and an imperial court far removed from the established Roman aristocracy and its power struggles.

ECONOMIC INTERESTS

Constantinople's location on important trade routes made it possible to promote the economic dynamism and wealth of the empire. Constantine invested heavily in the expansion and embellishment of the city, which quickly turned Constantinople into an economic, cultural and political center.

NEW CHRISTIAN CENTER

Constantine promoted Christianity as the state religion and Constantinople was to serve as the capital of this new Christian empire. The city was founded free of pagan traditions and symbolized the renewal and spiritual direction of the empire under Christian influence. Although the exact nature of Constantine's personal faith is a matter of debate, his support for Christianity was crucial to its spread and institutionalization in the Roman Empire.

DIVISION OF THE EMPIRE

After Constantine, the empire was often divided into Western and Eastern Roman empires, with their own emperors and administrations.

THE END OF THE WESTERN ROMAN EMPIRE

In the 5th century, the Western Roman Empire experienced further erosion of its political and military power due to invasions by Germanic tribes such as the Goths, Vandals and Huns. The traditional "fall" of the Western Roman Empire is dated to 476 AD, when the Germanic leader Odoacer deposed the last Western Roman emperor, Romulus Augustulus, and declared himself "King of Italy". Romulus is named after the founder of Rome, about whom we have already written in detail in this book.

"VANDALISM"

The word vandalism, which is still used today and means "destructive", originally comes from the raids of the Vandals, who plundered Rome in 455 AD. The Vandals were then defeated in 533 AD by the Byzantine general Belisar on behalf of the Roman Emperor Justinian, which meant the end of their kingdom.

THE HUNS

The Huns were a nomadic people from Central Asia who pushed their way into Europe in the 4th century AD. Their arrival led to the great migration of peoples and the fall of many Germanic tribes. They caused many problems for the Romans and contributed greatly to the fall of the Western Roman Empire.

ATTILA THE HUN

Attila, known as "Attila the Hun", was one of the most powerful and fearsome rulers of the Huns. He ruled from around 434 until his death in 453 AD and is known for his military campaigns against the Eastern Roman and Western Roman Empires. His most famous military campaign was the invasion of Western Europe in 451 AD, where he marched through Gaul (modern-day France) and encountered a coalition of Romans and Germanic tribes at the Battle of the Catalaunian Fields (also known as the Battle of Châlons). His death in 453 AD was followed by a rapid decline of the Huns, which shows how much their power and unity were linked to his leadership. Attila died under mysterious circumstances the night after his wedding. While some accounts speak of a violent death, most historians believe that he died of an internal hemorrhage.

THE BYZANTINE EMPIRE

This book deals primarily with the ancient Roman Empire, whose end is often marked by the fall of Rome in 476 AD. Here, however, is a brief insight into the Eastern Roman Empire.

The Eastern Roman Empire (often called the Byzantine Empire) lasted for almost 1,000 more years, until 1453 AD It had many distinctive features that set it apart from the earlier Roman Empire. While the Roman Empire was dominated by Latin, the Eastern Roman Empire was dominated by Greek language and culture. The Christian faith also played a major social and institutional role. The Eastern Roman Empire lived through almost the entire Middle Ages and was the most important pillar in the preservation and transmission of the ancient, in many aspects more progressive, culture and way of life at that time.

THE END OF THE BYZANTINE EMPIRE

The Fourth Crusade ended in 1204 with the conquest and sacking of Constantinople, which dealt the Eastern Roman Empire such a huge blow that it never recovered. Just under 150 years later, it came to its final end with the conquest of Constantinople by the Ottomans.

FACTS ABOUT
THE BYZANTINE EMPIRE

Fork scandal: When the Byzantine princess Theophanu used a fork in the 10th century, this caused a scandal in Italy. The use of forks was considered unnecessarily luxurious and against the natural order.

Mechanical throne: The Byzantine emperor Theophilos (829-842 AD) is said to have had a mechanical throne that could rise and fall, surrounded by singing golden birds and roaring golden lions to impress and intimidate visitors.

Secret firearms: The Byzantines used a secret weapon called "Greek fire", a flammable liquid that continued to burn even on water and was mainly used in naval battles. The exact composition of Greek fire remains a secret to this day.

GET INSIGHTS INTO ANOTHER BOOK YOU MIGHT LIKE:

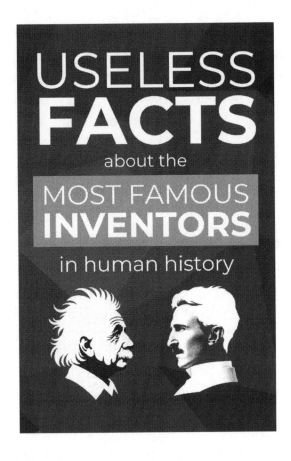

500+ FACTS ABOUT THE MOST FAMOUS INVENTORS

EXCITING FACTS
ABOUT THE FIRST BIKES

No horses: Early bikes were often pulled by oxen or donkeys, long before horses were domesticated and used for this purpose.

No nails: The first wheels and carriages were built without metal nails; instead, wooden dowels and tenon joints were used.

Wheels without roads: When the wheel was invented, there were no roads. The first carts were used on unpaved terrain, which was quite a challenge.

Development of the axle block: The invention of the axle block, in which the wheel rotated around a fixed axle, took place only a few years or decades after the wheel and was a significant advance and made movement more efficient.

LEONARDO DA VINCI

Leonardo da Vinci is usually "only" seen by the general public as an artist who, among other things, painted the most valuable picture of all time, the Mona Lisa. Most people forget his incredibly groundbreaking work in biology and mechanics, which is why we will focus heavily on it here. Da Vinci was one of the greatest autodidacts and polymaths who ever lived. Autodidacts are people who teach themselves everything through practice and experience, without teachers or mentors.

THE PERSON DA VINCI

Leonardo da Vinci was born on April 15, 1452 in Anchiano, a small village near Vinci, Italy. His full name was Leonardo di ser Piero da Vinci, which means 'Leonardo, son of Piero from Vinci'. His father, Ser Piero, was a wealthy notary and his mother, Caterina, was a young peasant woman. Leonardo was an illegitimate child, which at the time meant that, in addition to social exclusion, he had no formal rights to his father's property.

FIRST VENTURES

After completing his studies, Benz worked in various technical positions, gaining experience and expanding his knowledge in the fields of mechanical engineering and design. In 1871, he and August Ritter founded the company "Eisengießerei und mechanische Werkstätte" (Iron foundry and mechanical workshop) in Mannheim, which later specialized in the development of gas engines. After buying Ritter out of the partnership, he renamed the company "Gasmotoren-Fabrik Mannheim".

THE INVENTION OF THE CAR

Benz was fascinated by the idea of developing a motorized car. Despite financial setbacks and technical challenges, he never gave up on his vision. In 1885, he completed the construction of his first automobile, the "Benz Patent Motor Car Number 1". This three-wheeled vehicle was equipped with a single-cylinder four-stroke engine and a patent application was filed on January 29, 1886 (patent DRP 37435), which is considered the birth date of the modern automobile.

NIKOLA TESLA

After the most famous scientist, let's move on to probably the most famous inventor in the history of mankind. Nikola Tesla should be familiar to everyone, especially after Elon Musk named his car brand after him. For many, Tesla is more than just an inventor. He has probably been called everything from insane to genius. He is known for having invented things that were centuries before his time. Things that we still can't understand today and things that he probably took with him to his grave for all eternity.

THE PERSON TESLA

Tesla was idealistic, eccentric, had very strange habits and lived like a hermit. In other words, everything you wouldn't want to be. But he was definitely one thing: a genius. He was born on July 10, 1856 in the village of Smiljan, which at the time belonged to Austria-Hungary (now part of Croatia). Tesla was the fourth of five children of the priest Milutin Tesla and his wife Georgina. Like Einstein, he showed an extraordinary talent for mathematics and science from an early age.

The greatest inventors and thinkers in human history... What is their background story? What was their childhood like? How did these geniuses live? What made them so special? What routines did they have? In what circumstances did they develop their inventions and what motivated them?

What were their greatest inventions and how did they change the world for good? How was it possible to invent the light bulb or electricity in general? Who invented the aeroplane? Who invented the printing press? And what is behind all the millennia-old inventions, such as the wheel?

How did Einstein's E = mc² pave the way for the atomic bomb? How was Nikola Tesla able to invent things in the 19th century that are still inexplicable to us today? How was Leonardo da Vinci able to draw exact plans for a helicopter over 400 years before the first helicopter, while 'on the side' painting the Mona Lisa, the most valuable picture of all time?

The answers to all these questions and over 500 other facts are in this book and are just waiting to be discovered by you!

Just scan

Go directly to the book on Amazon now.

USELESS
FACTS
about the
MOST FAMOUS
INVENTORS
in human history

Made in the USA
Middletown, DE
14 June 2024

55812869R00077